Contents

Say Cheese!

*H*ello everybody. Wallace here. As it's raining cats and dogs outside (there are pets everywhere – that pesky weather machine has gone wrong *again*!), I thought this would be the perfect opportunity to dig out the old photo album and take a trip down memory lane. I remember what a fine head of hair I once had, before my automated-hairdresser got a bit out of hand... Our trusty camera has seen some fine moments over the years.

← *Baked by my own fair hands, that was one fantastic cheese-filled fondant fancy. I think little Gromit was a bit disappointed it wasn't filled with chocolate-covered doggie delights, weren't you lad? But as I pointed out at the time, why have chocolate when you can have cheese?*

There I am, → *so proud of the young lad and his Double First in Engineering for Dogs, a chip off the old block. Ah, and my last few wisps of hair. Think I still have those somewhere...*

There's nothing better than a good old British summer holiday in sunny Blackpool. We had a cracking time, didn't we lad? Gromit went a b green on this ride. I did warn him that three ic creams and a stick of candyfloss might not be the best pre-rollercoaster snack. Silly old poo

A grand day out this was, and well
worth the long trip to stock up the
pantry. How's a chap to survive without
his daily dose of cheese on toast?

A dog is a man's best friend, that's for sure.
Gromit knows exactly what's going to make
my birthday special – an extra large slice of my
favourite Wensleydale cheese. Thanks, lad.

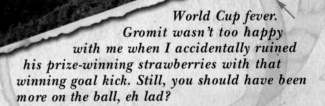

World Cup fever.
Gromit wasn't too happy
with me when I accidentally ruined
his prize-winning strawberries with that
winning goal kick. Still, you should have been
more on the ball, eh lad?

Now here was the start of an unexpected yet
otherwise delightful holiday. It began when I
was testing out my rain-repelling umbrella and
ended on a beach in South America. Just wish
I'd had a chance to pack my suitcase...

Wallace's Invisible Inventions Word-search

Time to sharpen your pencils, young inventors! Hidden in the grid below are names of some of the tools Wallace needs to build his amazing contraptions. We've also hidden the names of Wallace's most famous inventions in the grid too – can you find them all? The answers can go horizontally, vertically and diagonally – they may even be backwards! If you get stuck, the answers are on page 58. Good luck!

```
S C R A C K E R V A C F F J E C S L Y A
B O S D R F L M M T Y K N G H E P A R G
M H C L J O F I L A B O R A T O R Y E R
T R I C G E T J Y Q X O S V C B I H A A
W O E O A T P N D V B C L K N S N R D B
E R M G D M L Q E B R W S T U P G U B A
N E W S A U A E F V T E E E S R S O R T
S F A R E O N T G N N N M P J F T T E R
O Z L A T I S N I M E I C E R W J L F O
P S L I U S D T H C R H T I A S L I A N
E C A E S P A N N E R C Y R R Y S P D B
T R C W O A G U J R O A T W S C A A E F
F E H C O T U A L Y P M H C A W F S Y J
T W R I N E J O X U C R O S Y P Z B U T
D S O P F N L A S H O P I N A T O R L D
I T P L Y T A T I N E H G G B M M A I S
G O S H H D F H J K L E R T H G W I O V
E L D D P B E G R E A S E E W X R N Y H
T E C H N O T R O U S E R S G R O S O B
```

Words to find:

Tools
BOLTS
BRAINS
COGS
GREASE
INVENTOR
LABORATORY
MACHINE
NAILS
PATENT
PLANS
SCREWS
SPANNER
SPRINGS

Inventions
AUTOCHEF
CRACKERVAC
GRABATRON
SHOPINATOR
SOCCAMATIC
TECHNO TROUSERS
TELLYSCOPE

Gourmet Greats
Cheese on Toast

Is there any finer meal than Wensleydale on toast? If there is, I've never eaten it. So how do you make this king of meals? Well, first get your ingredients together...

INGREDIENTS (For one person and one dog)

1 hydraulic pump
4 feet small-bore copper piping
12 feet high-grade AC/DC electrical wiring
1 oxyacetylene torch
1 tungsten safety shield
300 cross-head screws
6-volt motor
100 4-hole 6-inch steel girders
2 cricket shin pads
1 bag mixed ball bearings
2 actuator units
1 angle-poise lamp (disassembled)
1 alarm clock (quartz)

This is to make a combined hydraulically powered bread thermaliser/cheese de-solidifier. Or you could just use a toaster and the grill in the oven.

OTHER INGREDIENTS

4 ozs (or as much as it takes to pile on 4 slices of toast) cheddar cheese (or Wensleydale!)
4 slices of bread (white, brown or granary)
fresh ground pepper
tomato ketchup
salt to taste

DIRECTIONS

Build combined hydraulically powered bread thermaliser/cheese de-solidifier.
Add bread and cheese.
Or...
Lightly toast bread.
Grate or slice cheese (if you're a nipper, ask an adult to help!).
Pile cheese on toast.
Put cheese on toast into oven on medium heat.
Grill until cheese has gone all soft and sticky, or until a delicious golden brown.

Cheese on Crackers

Another fine cheese-based meal. Again, Wensleydale is a key ingredient, although I admit on occasion I do like a bit of Gorgonzola.

INGREDIENTS

Crackers
Cheese

DIRECTIONS

Remove crackers from the packet.
Slice cheese (again, if you're a young'un, ask an adult to help!).
Place slices of cheese on the crackers.

TIP
Best consumed with a cup of tea, whilst wearing some nice comfy slippers.

IT'S THE MOST WONDERFUL TIME OF THE YEAR AT WEST WALLABY STREET...

Right, lad, have we got everything?

I've made a list. Don't make me check it *twice.*

WEST WALLABY ST.

Cheese? You've got the cheese? Not a proper dinner without some nice *cheese* to round it off.

And make sure you've got the present...

...we *have* to take a present. After all, it's not every day we get invited to such a *salubrious* event!

Lady Tottington requests the pleasure of the company of Wallace and Gromit at Tottington Hall for her annual Winter Solstice Feast.

Oh, I say, Gromit lad! I'm getting quite beside myself!

WHAT A CARVE UP!

Best bib and tucker! We're going to be moving in *very* fancy circles!

SAFE · SECURE · HUMANE
PEST CONTROL

ANTI-PESTO
S.W.A.T. TEAM

HOP 21T

Your ladyship, may I present Mr Wallace and Mr Gromit.

Ey up!

6

Story Dan Abnett · Art Brian Williamson and Bambos Georgiou · Colours John Burns · Letters Jimmy Betancourt/Comicraft

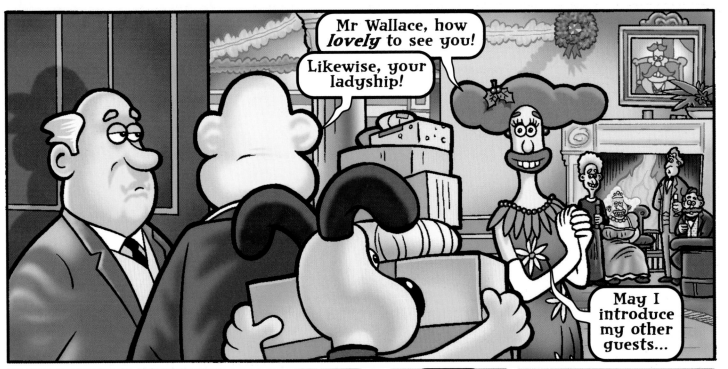

Mr Wallace, how *lovely* to see you!

Likewise, your ladyship!

May I introduce my other guests...

...Reverend Clement Hedges...

Oh, hello Wallace. How nice to see you.

...Lady Carthorse...

Aren't you that inventor chappie?

...Mr Roger Prim...

An inventor, you say? You mean, like a *manual worker?*

...and Colonel Muesli.

Little chap with him looks like a bally dog.

And how *sweet!* You've brought a present! Is it one of your clever inventions?

Oh, yes! It's the very *pinnacle* of clever!

But I think, for full effect, it would be best unwrapped at *dinner* time!

DINNER IS SERVED...

Oh, look everyone! The turkey's arrived!

It's time to unveil my gift, your ladyship! I took the liberty of setting it up for you...

...it's a *self-carving turkey!* You strap the exo-skeleton onto the roasted bird, stand back, and *hey presto!*

How very ingenious!

A *what* did he say?

I can't imagine!

Is it humane?

It's a bally party trick is what it is!

So... *hey presto!*

Eh?

It would appear that someone's *gobbled* the turkey.

Either that, or it's self-carved itself to the point of *obliteration.*

Yes, maybe it sliced itself *too* thinly.

I... I don't *understand!* What on *Earth's* going on?

I'll tell you what's bally going on. It's been *scoffed,* all right. Look at the *tooth marks* on the bones.

They as good as identify the culprit...

Your bally *dog,* sir! *He's* had away with the bally turkey!

Oh, I don't thin--

Well, dogs *do* like bones. It's an attested fact.

And tooth marks are fairly conclusive.

I'm very disappointed in you, Gromit.

Oh no! I won't have this! You can't go around accusing poor Gromit!

Those marks on the bones could just as easily have been made by a carving knife!

Why, if I had my soft x-ray machine with me, I could probably locate microscopic pieces of metal!

In fact, that's what I'll do! I'm going to use scientific methods of analysis to discover the *true* perpetrator of this dastardly crime!

Gromit, would you be so kind as to go to the van and fetch the detective kit?

Now then. Let's begin at the beginning.

I put it to you, Reverend Hedges, that at the time of the disappearance...

...*you* were in the library with the light refreshments...

...so, Mr Prim, at *the* precise moment the turkey vanished, *you* were in the snooker room.

Doing what, Mr Prim? Doing *what?*

Playing snooker.

Alone?

I find I win more *often* when I play alone.

Look, is your dog coming back or *what?*

9

...so the dog must be guilty, *must* he, Lady Carthorse?

It's got a dog's handiwork all *over* it, man!

Aha! But dogs don't *have* hands, *do* they?

Oh, *paws* then!

...

...How long *for*, exactly?

Oh!

Oh dear me! The game's up, isn't it?

You were quick to point the finger, Colonel.

Bally dog's a *bad sort.*

I --

Excuse me?

I do beg your pardon, your ladyship, but I feel I must confess...

The butler did it!

Well, not *me* exactly...

...but rather the *puppy* I bought as a *surprise gift* for her ladyship. He's a *spirited* little fellow, and he got to the turkey while it was resting in the kitchen.

Oh, never mind the *turkey!* He's *lovely!*

It's been so long since there's been a dog around the place!

Seems we owe you a bally apology, Wallace.

No harm done, Colonel.

There remains the question of *dinner,* your ladyship.

Well... we brought cheese for *afters,* but nothing beats a cracking *cheese soufflé!*

AND SO...

More soufflé, anyone?

Do tell us more about your fascinating job, Mr Wallace...

Yes, *inventor,* aren't you?

Oh, well, it's not *all* glamour, but there was *one* time...

Sounds bally interesting to me.

SEASON'S GREETINGS

11

A Right Good Yarn!

Wendolene Ramsbottom's Window on the Wonderful World of Wool.

Hello everybody.
Wendolene Ramsbottom here,
ready to unravel the mysteries of the
fascinating world of wool.
Wool has always held a special place in my heart.
It was wool that brought me and Wallace together.
Our eyes met across a ball of it. No.7 Wash 'n' go
3-ply I think it was, 'Burnt Crimson' if I remember rightly.
Now, when you think about where wool comes from, you
probably imagine fluffy little lambs frolicking in the
fields. Am I right? But that's not the only source
of this magical material. Try picturing a big,
hissing camel instead! I wouldn't fancy
getting too close when he's being sheared
(I bet he gets the hump)!
Let's find out more...

GLOSSARY OF THE KNITTING TERMS

Knitting Pulling: Loops through loops.
Needle: Your basic tool of the trade that comes in all manner of shapes and sizes.
Hook: Used for crochet. Also handy for removing chunks of cheese from your teeth, according to Wallace. Best to wash them after – unless you want to work cheese into your garment, and whilst Wallace might think this is an excellent idea, it's probably very unhygienic.
Knit One: A plain stitch.
Purl One: A plain stitch backwards (not the way it's said or doing it behind your back).
Tension: The tightness or looseness of your knitting. Also the feeling when Shaun's chewed up my knitting pattern.
Casting On: Making a new row of stitches.
Cast Off: Finishing off a final row of stitches. Also makes me think of sailing into the sunset with Wallace.

RABBIT

Type of wool: Angora

Origin: Found worldwide, but these fluffy little furballs are captive-bred – you won't find a wild one. Not unless it's one that's escaped, fallen in with the wrong crowd and is now 'punking-up' its look with spikes and plenty of processed-cabbage hair gel!

Description: This soft, fluffy wool can be spun from the clods of hair that are found in your rabbit's hairbrush – regular, gentle brushing usually does the trick, so long as it doesn't get fed up and hop it!

For/Against: Often mistaken for a small dog or nice pair of slippers. Needs a lot of brushing, grooming and nightmarish de-knotting.

Used for: Fluffy jumpers that don't sit well on the amply proportioned (I'm told). Important Knitting Tip: Wool from were-rabbits is notably sub-standard.

CAMEL

Type of wool: Camelhair

Origin: The two-humped Bactrian Camel of Mongolia

Description: This lightweight wool has thermostatic properties to keep you warm when it's cold and cool when it's hot, which can be very handy if you're prone to hot flushes, like me.

For/Against: The wool falls out in clumps in the moulting season, although it tends to be a bit on the scurfy side – very popular with birds, who love it for lining nests. However, just watch out for those teeth when you're bending down to collect it! Not sure Wallace's Knitmaster could cope with the humps. Or the spitting.

Used for: Classic camelhair coats. Wallace does cut a dash in his!

GOAT

Type of wool: Cashmere

Origin: Himalayan Kashmir Goat

Description: This silky-soft fibre is plucked from the goat's soft undercoat. Let's just hope they're not ticklish, but, just in case, always wear a crash helmet and cricket box. Or perhaps that's why it's so expensive – danger money! That and the fact you need a mountaineering expedition just to collect the wool.

For/Against: A royal banquet for moths – so needs a good shake out once a week. A bit like Wallace's wallet!

Used for: Outrageously expensive jumpers. Nice to wear but hardly worth giving up tank tops and a year's supply of Wensleydale for.

ALPACA

Type of wool: Funnily enough, Alpaca

Origin: Deepest, darkest Peru. For those a little rusty with their geography, that's in South America.

Description: This fine, soft fibre was a cherished treasure of the ancient Inca Civilisation, which was, ooh, ever such a long time ago. Don't ask me exactly when, I'm a bit woolly! (hehe!)

For/Against: These gentle creatures look like someone stretched a sheep or shrunk a camel (or perhaps both at the same time). However, they have no horns, nipping incisors, hooves or claws, which is a big plus in my book.

Used for: Nice soft jumpers that make lovely presents for Christmas, birthdays, anniversaries, any excuse really.

GET CRACKING

CRACKING CONUNDRUM

Solve the clues below and put your answers into the grid. When you're finished, the letters in the green squares spell out one of Wallace and Gromit's greatest fears:

1. If Wallace said 'bonjour' instead of 'hello', he would be speaking which language? (6)

2. The name of Wallace & Gromit's detective agency is Anti-what? (5)

3. One of Wallace's favourite meals is cheese on what? (5)

4. Wallace's favourite pastime (9)

5. Wallace has one of these at the bottom of his garden (4)

6. Wallace often enjoys a cup of what? (3)

7. What sort of day out did Wallace & Gromit have? (5)

8. A sheep who wears a pullover (5)

CHEESEY PICKLE

Wallace can't work out which cheeses he has stashed away in his fridge! Can you unscramble the letters and help him find out?

REDCHAD _____   DEWSLAYLEEN _____

STONILT _____   HRESIHEC _____

MADE _____   ERIB _____

LOZLEARAZM _____   EDR ETRIEESLC _____

14

KRIS-CROSS

INVENTIONS

NOW TURN
TO PAGE 58
FOR THE
ANSWERS!

3 Letters
CUP
TEA

4 Letters
TOOL

5 Letters
FOOTY
ROBOT

6 Letters
GROMIT
MARROW
CHEESE

7 Letters
WALLACE

8 Letters
MEATABIX
SLIPPERS
DOGWARTS

9 Letters
ANTIPESTO

10 Letters
SNOOZATRON
~~INVENTIONS~~

Wallace is famous for his cracking contraptions, but did you know that he also likes to invent crafty puzzles for Gromit to solve too? His latest is this peculiar crossword – with a difference! There are no clues – all you need to do is put the words listed below into the correct place on the grid. We've put one of the words in to start you off. At the end, you should have one word left over. Can you work out which one it is?

HOME SWEET HOME!

How do. Wallace here. Ay-Up! magazine have been on at me to let them take a tour of 62 West Wallaby Street ever since my (sorry, lad) Gromit's giant cabbage won first prize at the village fete. Ah, the terrible burdens of fame and fortune…

Poor Gromit was thrown out of his room by that pesky penguin – but we got him in the end, didn't we lad?

Gromit objects to sharing a bathroom with Shaun, who does get a bit mucky with all that messing about in fields. But someone has to clean the bathroom and when would I find the time?

put the odd emergency slice of cheese on toast under the grill when Gromit decides I'm getting a little porky and starts putting celery instead of cheese in my sandwiches. I should do the same with his chocolate-covered doggy delights, if only I knew where he kept them...

Also home to my fantastic dressing machine and breakfast-maker. Helps get those inventing brain cells into gear of a morning.

Gromit's favourite room, I believe, and he's in charge. A busy inventor like me doesn't have time for cooking, except to

Just the ticket! The perfect place t put my feet up with a nice cup of and a crossword. And the ideal pl to fully appreciate the odd snack cheese and crackers...

Secret! Don't tell Gromit, but when he does decide to put me on a diet there's always my secret cheese stash hidden away in the bookcase...

My favourite room, where I create my many mostly successful and always amazing inventions. I'm currently working on a sensational, top-secret machine for Lady Tottington...

Gromit's greenhouse, home to his many prize-winning vegetables. What's it going to be next year, eh lad? A giant potato? Well, best get cracking or Mrs Appleby'll pip you to the post.

Our delightful garden, ideal for an afternoon of concentrated inventing in the hammock. That's thinking, not sleeping, thank you Gromit!

Gromit likes to keep our borders neat and watered. Cracking job, Gromit.

ROAD TRIP

62 WEST WALLABY STREET...

It's like I always say, *Gromit,* wherever I wander...

... there's no place like *home!*

It's a rare honour, being invited to give a talk at Lord Locan's *School For Precocious Upstarts.*

Good thing we have no trouble with the short notice, eh?

Ever ready, that's us!

Right then, Gromit — get that *show and tell* stuff stowed properly...

18 | Writer Simon Furman | Art Jimmy Hansen | Inks Bambos Georgiou | Colours John Burns | Letters Jimmy Betancourt/Comicra

... and get the *kettle* on!

No time for a *sit-down* breakfast, we've a long drive ahead of us.

So... we'll have it *on the go!*

Oh, and one more little improvisation... the *home-xpress* comes with an *autopilot* facility, for tricky manoeuvring and parking. Here...

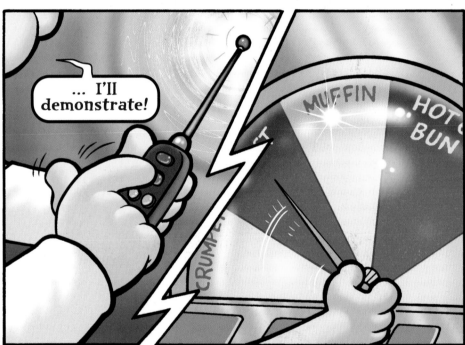

... I'll demonstrate!

Oo-er...

SCREECHHHHH

... it's not supposed to do *that!*

HONK HONK HONK

HOOOONK!

HONK

SREEE! VREEK

Shriek!

DRRING DRRING DRRING

DRRING DRRING

DRRING

Gromit? It's *Wallace.* listen carefully...

...Something's interfering with the *signal* from the remote control.

21

The radio frequencies must be cancelling each other out. Gromit...

... try *changing* the station...

Well done, Gromit. I think you've—

Oo er...

CONTINUED ON PAGE 32!

23

WHERE'S WALLACE?

Oh dear! My wash-and-go washing machine has ruined a perfectly good piece of fashionable knitwear! What's happened to all the lovely colours? Can you help brighten up my look?

That's it!
Now I'm a total knockout

Amazing MAZE!

Can you help the hungry Were-rabbit get to Gromit's greenhouse and a delicious giant vegetable dinner? Shh, don't tell Gromit...

DOG & CLONE

MAKE YOUR OWN COPY OF GROMIT!

IN WHICH CASE IT IS ALL THE WORK OF GROMIT

Hello there

Having not quite got to grips with the whole DNA thingy, I have concluded that, for now, there are simpler ways to clone Gromit.

All you have to do is use the blank grid below to make a perfect copy of my chum and inventing companion. Have fun, whilst I get back to my copy of *What Gene? The Beginners Guide to Cloning and Genetic Plagiarism...*

WHICH WALLACE & GROMIT CHARACTER DO YOU MOST RESEMBLE?

Hello there! Gromit's just popped out to the supermarket to fetch me some delicious Wensleydale after my last invention, the Shopper 13, decided to go a bit barmy and lose me cheese! Fancy taking his place for him in my new experiment? I've just built a contraption called THE PERSONALITRON-3000, which can detect your character with a 0.0798% margin of error. You'll do it? **Smashing!**

INPUT THE CORRECT ANSWERS BELOW:

It's breakfast time, and you've come downstairs to an empty kitchen table. What do you do next?

A. Spend all day building a machine that brews a piping-hot pot of tea for two, freshly buttered toast with a selection of jams, and three perfectly boiled eggs with soldiers so you'll never have this problem again!_____ ■

B. Prepare a breakfast from whatever food you have in the house, or failing that, visit the supermarket for supplies._____ ■

C. Graze on the nearest door._____ ■

D. Go round to your neighbours and eat them out of house and home, while in disguise._____ ■

E. Call up a friend, and ask if they can feed you, just this once!_____ ■

28

It's a Sunday evening, and you're sitting in the lounge with your feet up, reading a magazine. Which magazine would you prefer to read from the following?

A. Ay-Up!_____ ■

B. Total Vegetable_____ ■

C. What Lawn?_____ ■

D. Cool Crooks Quarterly_____ ■

E. Wool-Wearers Weekly_____ ■

What would your ideal holiday destination be from the following list?

A. The Moon_____ ■

B. The annual Carrot Festival, France_____ ■

C. A nice hill in Dorset_____ ■

D. The North Pole_____ ■

E. Woolwich_____ ■

A new exhibition of ancient Egyptian treasures has opened at your local museum. Do you:

A. Stay at home, because there's important work to be done on a new invention you've dreamed up.___ ■

B. Make sure you're first in line for a ticket._____ ■

C. Get thrown out of the museum for chewing on the exhibits.___ ■

D. Start plotting how you're going to make off with the treasure.___ ■

E. Book tickets for two, and invite a local inventor to join you.___ ■

Your friend has invited you to a sports event in town. Which will you be watching first?

A. Cheese Football_____ ■

B. Bows and Marrows_____ ■

C. International Speed Dining___ ■

D. The 100-metre dash_____ ■

E. Ballroom dancing_____ ■

ANSWERS:

Mostly A's

YOU ARE

WALLACE!

Mostly B's

YOU ARE

GROMIT!

Mostly C's

YOU ARE

SHAUN!

Mostly D's

YOU ARE

FEATHERS!

Mostly E's

YOU ARE

WENDOLENE!

101 Uses For A Nice Bit of Wensleydale

(Well, 10 for starters, anyway!)

Hello everybody. Wallace here, with some excellent ideas for the leftover cheese that you may find lingering in your pantry, or evolving its own intelligence at the bottom of the fridge. Now, you may well think the only thing Wensleydale is good for is popping on a cracker whenever hunger calls, but you'd be wrong! Oh, yes, you'd be amazed what a versatile substance cheese can be, given the right conditions and a free-thinking mind. Here are some of my favourite uses:

1 PROP FOR A TABLE LEG

Do you have a table that suffers from uneven leg length distribution? Suffer no more! Simply pop a surgically-shaped wedge or specially-sized block of Wensleydale underneath the offending leg, and you will no longer need to live in fear or suffer the humiliation of hot porridge sliding into your lap!

2 EAR MUFFS

If, like me, you're sometimes kept awake at night by the caterwauling of the local feline population, I find a cup-shaped slice of Wensleydale pressed firmly over each ear does the trick. This clam-shaped covering also has the same effect of a seashell, bringing to life the soothing sounds of the sea. May lead to missing your early morning alarm call.

3 BATH SPONGE

Many's the time I've gone to give Gromit his bath, only to find that his sponge has disappeared! I've discovered a bit of Wensleydale makes an excellent substitute, although if too dry, it can crumble and clog up the plughole. And forget all this pomegranate, honeysuckle and bandicoot foaming bath moisturiser. What better way to feel fresh and clean than with the great smell of cheese?

4 TOOTHPASTE

Out of Pearl-o-Brite? Fear not, for a smidge of my specially patented Cheesy Grin toothpaste applied to your molars will do you the world of good! Its active bacteria extract coats your teeth in a waxy yellow film to protect it from all manner of nasty plaque and decay. It will also make them gleam with cheesy freshness and give you a golden smile!

5 FISH BAIT

What better way to spend a day than messing about on the river (or seashore. Or lake. Or reservoir, for that matter)? Gromit and I often take to the waves (well, ripples actually) and set out to catch us a monster. Try a few crumbs of the yellow stuff as bait and Bob's your uncle – the fish are fairly flinging themselves onto your hook. There's also the added bonus that if your boat springs a leak, a wodge of Wensleydale will soon bung up the hole!

6 CLOCK

I know, I know, you think I'm losing my marbles, telling the time with cheese. But when the weight from the pendulum in my grandfather clock mysteriously went missing, a chunk of cheese was just the ticket to keep it ticking, without skipping a beat! Just watch out for mice.

7 PICTURE FRAME

For any of you creative types, here's a challenge: try carving an ornamental picture frame from a simple block of cheese. Just the thing to set off any ancestral portraits you may have lurking in the loft (or alternatively, that funny picture of your Auntie Nora, which is sure to bring a lemon tinge to her cheeks!).

8 HEIGHT EXTENDERS

If you are a little on the short side, pop a wedge of cheese into the heel of each shoe, and you'll soon be towering above the competition. And if you weren't lucky enough to have a nice, cheesy aroma wafting from your tootsies before, you will have now!

9 ROMANTIC GIFT

You've probably heard the phrase, 'say it with flowers', but I say, 'say it with cheese'! After all, what use is a bunch of daffodils that is going to keel over and die as soon as they've given you hay fever? No, take it from a man who knows – the way to a woman's heart is with Wensleydale.

10 GAME COUNTERS

The last time Gromit and I settled down for a nice game of draughts calamity struck! Several counters were missing, believed rolled down the crack in the floorboards. But no worries - some thin slices of Wensleydale and Lancashire, and a biscuit cutter were all that were needed. And our game had the added advantage of being able to eat your opponent's counters as you captured them. Grand!

SPECIAL NOTE

The suggestions in this article are intended to be solely of a humorous nature and should not be tried at home.

CONTINUED FROM PAGE 23!

He's in the *mega-mart!* And, oh...

... *that's* a good offer. We're a bit low on *double gloucester!*

Eeh. Well...

...waste not, want not! We'll take the *lot!* Ta very much.

33

Eh! I've a got a clear signal! Gromit must have *fixed* the problem. Well, lad...

... I'm *back* in charge!

Gromit!

I can't stop you in time! do something...

... *anything!*

KLK!

ZZRRTCH

WHOOF

Ah, um. Well...

... at least you've got some *drag!*

LATER...

Excellent talk, Wallace, *excellent.* Care to join us for a spot of lunch.

Oh, er... no, thank you...

...we'd better be getting back. Long drive and all that. We'll eat lunch *in transit.*

Ah, mm...

"... ANYONE SEEN *GROMIT?*"

JOURNEY'S END!

GET CRACKING

Someone's been at me cheese!

What a shocking calamity! I was feeling a bit peckish, so I went to the fridge for a nice bit of Wensleydale and found nothing left but a few measly crumbs! What a carry on! Help me find the culprit by solving the puzzle and crackin' the code below.

INSTRUCTIONS

Help Wallace solve the mystery of the missing Wenselydale by finding the names of these cheeses in the grid. They could be written horizontally, vertically or diagonally. When you have found all the varieties of cheese, work out which letters in the cheese names have been replaced with symbols. These letters are an anagram of the name of the culprit. Unscramble the letters and find out who has been at Wallace's cheese!

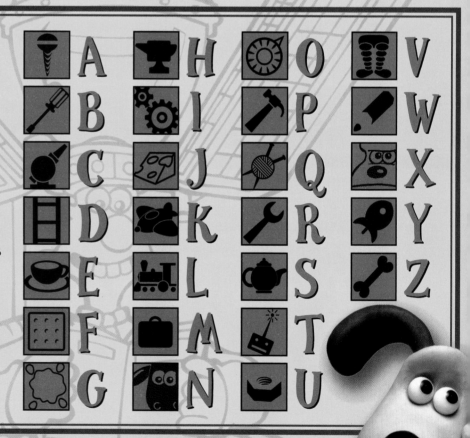

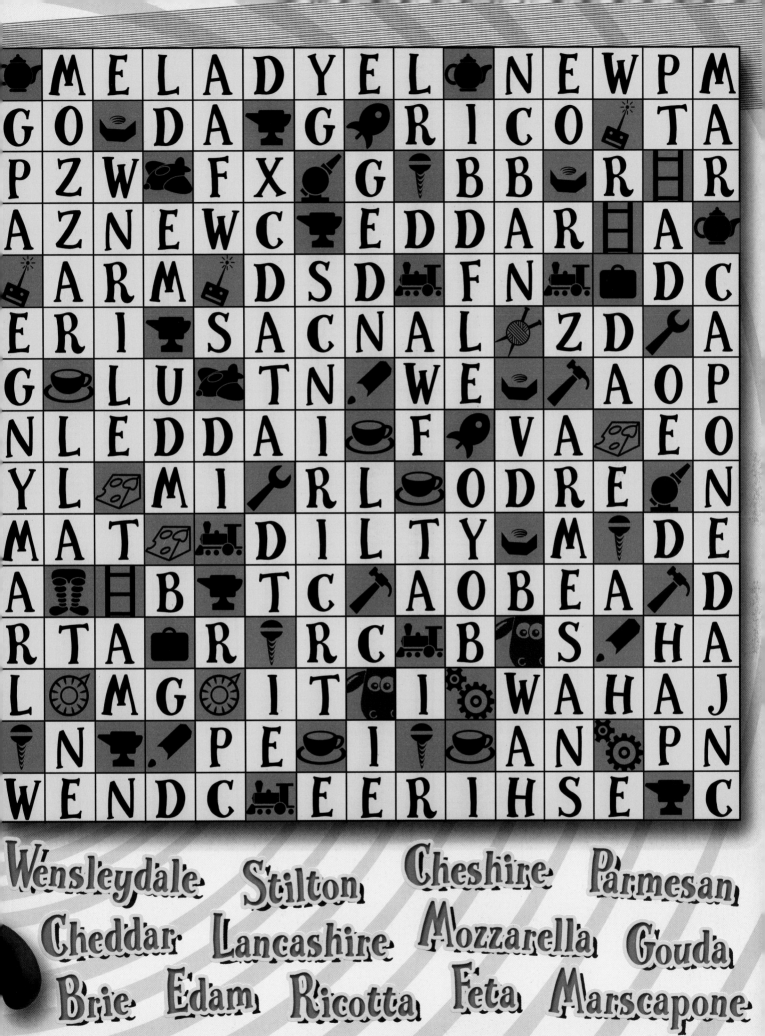

Wensleydale Stilton Cheshire Parmesan
Cheddar Lancashire Mozzarella Gouda
Brie Edam Ricotta Feta Marscapone

See page 58 for the answer...

37

TEST YOUR Wallace & Gromit KNOWLEDGE

How well do you think you know Wallace and Gromit?
Test yourself with our fantastic quiz and find out!

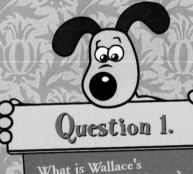

Question 1.

What is Wallace's favourite type of cheese?

a) Edam
b) Cheddar
c) Wensleydale

Question 2.

What is printed on Gromit's bedroom wallpaper?

a) Cheese
b) Bones
c) Rockets

Question 3.

What is the number of the house Wallace and Gromit live in on West Wallaby Street?

a) 62
b) 63
c) 52

Question 4.

What item does Feathers McGraw use to disguise himself with in *The Wrong Trousers*?

a) A false moustache on his face
b) A rubber glove on his head
c) A pair of clown shoes on his feet

Question 5.

What is the name of the mischievous rabbit in *The Curse of the Were-rabbit*?

a) Hitch
b) Hatch
c) Hutch

Question 6.

How many words has Gromit spoken in total?

a) None at all!
b) Only one!
c) He won't stop talking, that dog

Question 7.

What is the name of Wallace's love interest from *A Close Shave*?

a) Wendolene
b) Windy Sheen
c) Mavis Breen

Question 8.

Which of the following is NOT a Wallace & Gromit adventure?

a) *A Grand Day Out*
b) *The Wrong Trousers*
c) *The Stinky Cheese Mystery*

Question 9.

What is the name of Wallace & Gromit's S.W.A.T Team?

a) Anti-pasti
b) Anti-pesto
c) Auntie Peggy

Question 10.

What sort of giant vegetable did Gromit grow in *The Curse of the Were-rabbit*?

a) A carrot
b) A sprout
c) A marrow

Answers on page 59!

39

SAFE·SECURE·HUMANE
PEST CONTROL
Tel.2143
ANTI-PESTO
S.W.A.T. TEAM

SHAUN'S WORLD!

Hello there! Wallace here again. You'd think Shaun would want to introduce his very own page wouldn't you? But he much prefers munching his way through the contents of my lounge than telling you about his favourite things, so he's asked me to speak for him... Oh crikey! He's eating me phone book! Hang on Shaun! At least leave W for Wallace!

FLEECY FACT
One mature ewe produces seven to ten pounds of newly shorn wool a year – enough to make a man's suit.

BAA HA HA!
Q: Why did the sheep say "moo"?

A: It was learning a new language!

FLEECY FACT
Sheep have poor eyesight but an excellent sense of hearing.

BAA HA HA!
Q: What do sheep do on sunny days?

A: Have a baa – baa – cue!

FLEECY FACT
Altogether there are about 36 million sheep in the UK.

BAA HA HA!
Q: What do you get if you cross a sheep with a kangaroo?

A: A woolly jumper!

BAA HA HA!
Q: What do you call a sheep with no legs or head?

A: A cloud!

40

FLEECY FACT
One pound of wool can be spun into 20 miles of fine yarn.

BAA HA HA!
Q: Why was the lamb told off for being rude?

A: He would not say "thank ewe" to his mum!

BAA HA HA!
Q: What did the well-mannered sheep say to his friend at the field gate?

A: "After ewe!"

BAA HA HA!
Q: What do you get if a sheep walks under a cloud?

A: A sheep that's under the weather!

BAA HA HA!
Q: Why did Little Bo Peep lose her sheep?

A: She had a crook with her!

FLEECY FACT
The UK produces 1% of the world's raw wool, approximately 50,000 tonnes per year.

BAA HA HA!
Q: Where do sheep go for haircuts?

A: To the Baa-Baa shop!

FLEECY FACT
With approximately 11 million sheep, Wales accounts for about 15% of all sheep in the European Community.

FLEECY FACT
You might think that New Zealand has the most sheep per capita in the world, but while New Zealand only boasts 20 sheep per person, on the Falkland Isles there are over 700,000 sheep to 2,000 people – 350 each!

BAA HA HA!
Q: Which side of a sheep has the most wool?

A: The Outside!

SHAUN'S SHEEPY SNACKS

Shaun eats a very varied diet, as you can see from this selection!

Household Plants (any within chewing distance)
Porridge Boxes (much tastier than porridge)
Newspapers (The Daily Bugle is especially tasty)
Foot-rests
Magazines (all varieties)
Picture Frames
Comfy Chairs
Tea Cups
Dog Bones (especially Gromit's)
Cheese (especially Wallace's)

STRANGE FOOD FROM AROUND THE GLOBE

Look at some of the unusual delicacies people eat in different countries around the world!

Brazil: Dried Bananas – tiny sweet fruits
China: Durian – the smelliest fruit in the world, as big as a football, with a spiky shell
England: Jellied Eels – a traditional dish from the East End of London
Germany: Bierkase – a smelly cheese made from yeast
France: Snails – served in a garlic butter, a popular delicacy
Japan: Sushi – raw fish, often served on sticky rice with seaweed
Korea: Sea Slugs – served in little cups, and has a crunch like radishes
Philippines: Sweetcorn ice cream – an unusual, crunchy and cool dessert!
USA: Chicken's Feet – served extra spicy

SHEEPISH!

MAKE YOUR OWN SHAUN THE SHEEP!

STAR OF A CLOSE SHAVE

Settle down with a nice cup of tea, a plate of your favourite biscuits, and a few simple materials, and in no time you'll rustle up a little woolly friend of your very own.

You will need:

1 Cardboard
2 White wool
3 Scissors
4 2 black pipe cleaners
5 Black felt
6 Stick-on eyes

Always remember to ask an adult if you're using scissors or glue!

42

To make the pom pom:

Cut two rings of cardboard exactly the same size. Draw around a teacup to get the size of the outer ring, and a 2p coin for the inner ring.

2. Put the rings together. Cut a length of wool about a metre long. Hold one end on the outside of the ring and thread the other end through the hole, round the back and through the front again.

3. Keep wrapping the wool round in this way till all the cardboard is covered with several layers and the hole in the middle is very small. You will need to add more lengths of wool as you go.

4. Carefully cut through the wool around the outside edge of the ring.

5. Pass a piece of wool between the cardboard rings, around all the strands of wool and tie it tightly together.

6. To make the legs, take the black pipe cleaners and wrap them around this central knot. Twist them together, leaving the four legs poking out.

7. Remove the card, cutting it off if necessary. Fluff out the sheep's body, position the legs and bend the ends into hoof shapes.

8. Cut a face shape out of the black felt using the template printed here as a guide. Glue or stick on the eyes, and add a few loops of wool to the top of the head. Then glue the face to the pom pom. And there you have it, one fluffy sheep – not ba-a-ad!

Template

Some naked truths about our woolly friends:

According to the Chinese zodiac, if you were born in 1931, 1943, 1955, 1967, 1979, 1991 or 2003 you are a sheep! Other telltale signs might be a dislike of getting your feet wet, an inexplicable fear of dogs and a tendency to bleat on about things!

They may all look the same to you, but sheep have different faces and recognise each other, even after years apart. There's no pulling the wool over their eyes!

During the First World War U.S. President Woodrow Wilson kept sheep on the White House lawn and sold their wool to raise money for the Red Cross. Probably freed up his Sunday mornings too, with the lawnmowing taken care of!

New Zealand farmers have to pay a "fart tax" because of the methane gas (which damages the ozone layer) produced by their millions of sheep!

Egyptians believed rams were sacred and mummified them when they died – a thought almost as terrifying as were-rabbits!

THE *GROUX MANOR* ESTATE AND GROUNDS...

THMM DRRRT THMM!

THMM SKRRKZZZTT THMM DRRRT

HOODWINKED!

Well, Gromit lad, what do you think of my *"chalet valet?"* D.I.Y... au naturale.

The countryside...

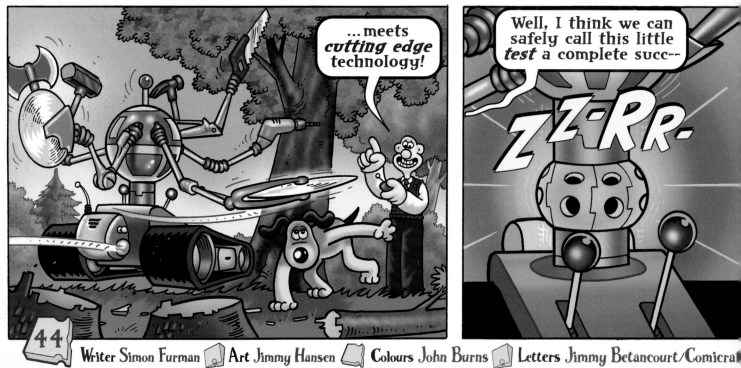

...meets *cutting edge* technology!

Well, I think we can safely call this little *test* a complete succ--

ZZ-RR-

44

Writer Simon Furman ◊ Art Jimmy Hansen ◊ Colours John Burns ◊ Letters Jimmy Betancourt/Comicra

BRRKTA BRRKTA

Oo-er. That's—*ow*—not right! Decorative *acorn* pebbledashing is the—*ee*—last stage of the process—*ow!*

BRRKTA FRZ BRRKTA ZZG

Something must have gummed up the works! *Gromit* –

– *DO* something!

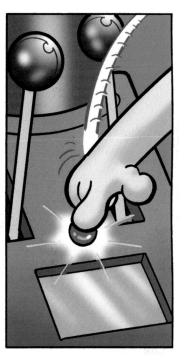

KFF! SPTT

Picnickers! I tell you, Gromit...

...some people have no *respect* for the countryside!

45

SOON...

Aha, *Wallace!*

Still a few *bugs* in the system to work out, mm?

A rogue metallic element in the works, *Gordon,* easily sorted.

Just need to *upgrade* the waste management grinders and it'll be ready for *anything!*

Mm-hm. Yes. Mm...

Well now, let's not keep the *others* waiting.

So everyone's arrived then?

Mais *non!* Anyone who's *anyone,* perhaps... the crème de la crème, certainly... but "everyone"...

...most certainly *not!*

SLAMM!

INSIDE...

Ladies and gentlemen!

TING A TING A TING!

As your duly elected chairperson, I, *Gordon Groux,* do solemnly declare...

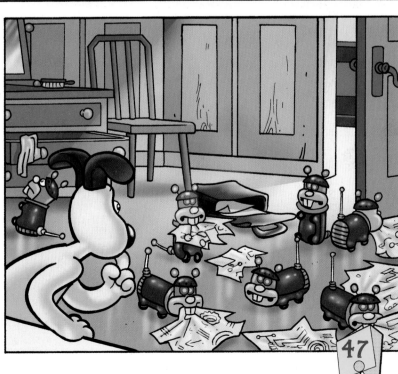

Now then, mon Petit Foragers...

48

...what *booty* have you brought me?

A *chameleon* boat, eh? Perfect. I know some contractors who'll be willing to pay *plenty* for that...

...with the right, ah, *optional extras!*

Cockle's boat, *Hurley's* pneumatic pogostick, *Wallace's* field-assembly apparatus...

...all right under my own roof, ripe for *exploitation!*

Well, *well...*

...a spy. Or should that be...

"...fall guy!"

Someone's *rifled* me drawers, Wallace! And Hurley's blueprints are missing too!

But... *who* could have *done* such a thing?

Gromit!

I think...

CRASH!

...we've *found* our miscreant!

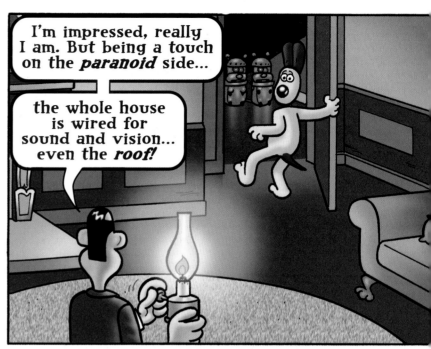

I'm impressed, really I am. But being a touch on the *paranoid* side...

the whole house is wired for sound and vision... even the *roof!*

And on the subject of home security...

...I believe you've *met* my *robo-gophers!* Much, *much* more than meets the eye!

OUTSIDE...

There! Much better. No *tin can* is going to get the better of my chalet-valet now--

G-Gromit? But...

...weren't you-?

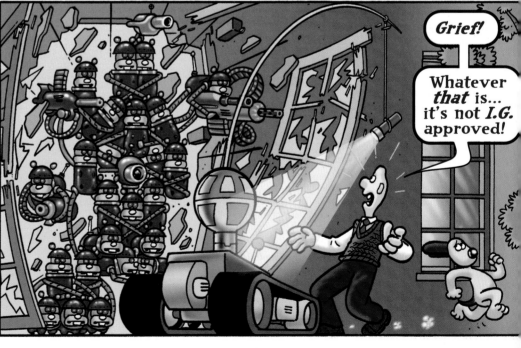

Grief!

Whatever *that* is... it's not *I.G.* approved!

Always a *stickler* for the rules, aren't you, Wallace? Shame. A little more, ah, flexibility...

...and, like me, you could have made a *mint* from munitions!

M-*munitions!* You... *scoundrel,* Groux! This... goes against everything the *I.G.* stands for!

Got to think *big,* Wallace...

Big, eh? Well...

VRRRTAK!

ZZR RTCH! SKUNNCH!

...it's high time *someone* cut you down to size!

SHRRSHHH

Oh dear.

LATER...

Ladies and gentlemen. My first act, as your *new* duly elected chairperson...

...is to formally *expel* one Gordon Groux, for numerous infractions of the *I.G.* code.

RIIIP

Hear, *hear!*

Right. Inventions *ahoy...*

Anyone seen *Gromit?* It's not like him...

"... to miss out on all the *excitement!*"

MEETING ADJOURNED!

53

GET CRACKING
SCRAMBLED CHEESE ON TOAST

How many times can you find the word CHEESE hidden in the scrambled letters below?

```
E R T D E S K B Z P O P X Q D F L
S P C R A K E E G R O W C E F H C
E V E H U T S Q A S W H B H L M O
E M O K L O E L M N O K C H E E C M
H E S E L B E E P P R X S O O N E C W
C L E A F B H H D C H E Z S E E S C
H E E C I O C H E M K L I O F H H E
C N L Y H U N O A E I O N E E R E W
P C J K F X J O C H Y H U K I C L E
```

WENDOLENE'S WOOLLY WIND-UP

Follow the strands of wool to match the person with their favourite thing!

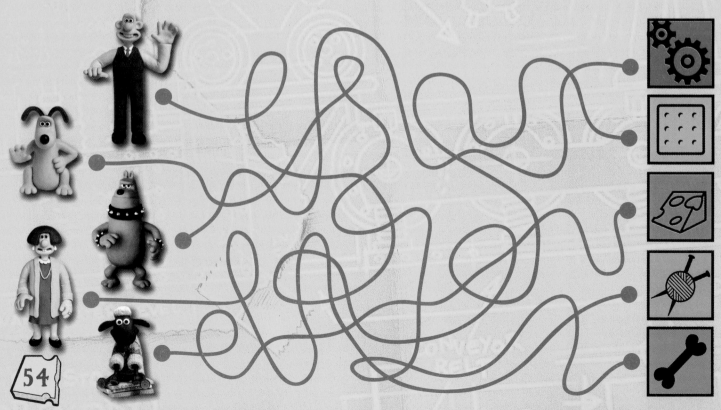

54

PC MACKINTOSH'S SLEUTHOKU

Help clueless PC Mackintosh solve this confounded conundrum! It's easy — each little box must contain the numbers 1 to 4, and these numbers must appear once on each line, horizontally and vertically. The tricky part is you aren't allowed to repeat a number on the same line! If you get stuck, the answers are on page 63!

1			
	2		3
		4	
2	4		

NOW TURN TO PAGE 59 FOR THE ANSWERS!

WALLACE'S TEA-BREAK CROSSWORD

Fill in the grid using the clues below!

Across
2 Gromit flew one of these in *The Curse of the Were-rabbit* (5)
4 Wallace uses this to hit nails with (6)
6 The Wrong ————— (8)
7 A Grand ——— ——— (3,3)
8 Gromit and Einstein are considered to be this (6)
10 One of Anti-pesto's inventions for capturing rabbits (6)
13 Wallace and Gromit flew one of these to the moon to fetch some cheese (6)
16 PC ————————, the friendly policeman (10)
18 Feathers' surname (6)
19 Into this, did Wallace transform (10)

Down
1 Gromit loves some of this on his toast! (3)
2 Wallace's favourite football team (7-5-3); see 9 down
3 Mmm, lovely with a cup of tea! (8)
5 You may have seen Wallace riding one of these! (9)
8 Unscramble this: D G N A R (5)
9 See 2 down
11 The penguin's first name (8)
12 You can see this at night, and it's made of cheese! (4)
14 You may drink a cup of this in the afternoon (3)
15 A favourite of Wendolene (4)
17 The ————— of the Were-rabbit (5)

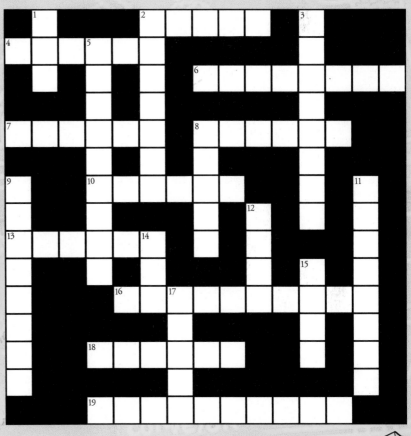

Wallace & Gromit's BRILLIANT BOARD GAME

You need counters and a dice and then you can get cracking! Good luck!

Lady Tottington invites you to tea, **miss a turn** while you munch on cucumber sandwiches.

You help Wallace & Gromit solve the missing marrows mystery, move **forward three places!**

Wallace lends you his pogostick, bounce **forward four places.**

Preston nearly catches up with you, move **back three places!**

The rocket is heading for the moon, jump aboard and fly **forward four places!**

Wallace gives you a lift in his motorbike's sidecar, drive **forward three places.**

You win Lady Tottington's cake competition, move **forward two places!**

You stop to help Gromit clear up after Shaun, **miss a go.**

Feathers has trapped you in the Techno Trousers, march **back five places!**

START HERE!

You become the Were-rabbit and hop **forward two places.**

Shaun shows you a short cut, move **forward two places.**

WELL DONE!

You're the winner!

PC Mackintosh takes you in for questioning about missing marrows, **miss a go.**

Feathers is lying in wait, go **back three places** to hide!

Gromit picks you up in his plane and flies you **forward four places!**

Wallace wants to show you his latest invention, **miss a go** while you take a look.

Shaun has lost his woolly jumper! **Miss a go** while you help him find it!

Watch out Preston's on the loose, run **back two places!**

Gromit shows you a short cut, move **forward one place.**

Shaun saves you from Preston, move **forward two places.**

Victor Quartermaine stops you for a chat, run **back three places** to escape!

You help Wallace solve the mystery of the missing gnome, move **forward four places!**

Wallace gives you a lift in the Anti-Pesto van, move **forward two places.**

Shaun's eaten your slippers, **miss a go** while you find new ones!

You stop to help Wendolene sort out a pile of wool, **miss a go.**

Shaun distracts Feathers, run **forward three places**

Cyberdog's about to catch up with you, run **back two places!**

You slip on a cup of tea, move **back one place.**

The rocket launches you **forward three places!**

ALL IS REVEALED!

Page 4: WALLACE'S INVISIBLE INVENTIONS WORD-SEARCH

```
S C R A C K E R V A C F F J E C S L Y A
B O S D R F L M M T Y K N G H E P A R G
M H C L J O F I L A B O R A T O R Y E R
T R I C G E T J Y Q X O S V C B I H A A
W O E O A T P N D V B C L K N S N R D B
E R M G D M L Q E B R W S T U P G U B A
N E W S A U A E F V T E E E S R S O R T
S F A R E O N T G N N N M P J F T T E R
O Z L A T I S N I M E I C E R W J L F O
P S L I U S D T H C R H T I A S L I A N
E C A E S P A N N E R C Y R R Y S P D B
T R C W O A G U J R O A T W S C A A E F
F E H C O T U A L Y P M H C A W F S Y J
T W R I N E J O X U C R O S Y P Z B U T
D S O P F N L A S H O P I N A T O R L D
I T P L Y T A T I N E H G G B M M A I S
G O S H H D F H J K L E R T H G W I O V
E L D D P B E G R E A S E E W X R N Y H
T E C H N O T R O U S E R S G R O S O B
```

Page 15: KRIS-CROSS
The missing word is FOOTY.

```
                              C
                              U
        A N T I P E S T O     P
            O         N
            O         O       G
    R       L         O       R
    O D O G W A R T S L        O
    B                 I        M
    O           I N V E N T I O N S
    T       M   P          R   I
            E   P   A R    O   T E A
            T   E   O      N
        M A R R O W
            A   S   W
            B       A
            I       L
            X       L
                    A C H E E S E
                    C
                    E
```

Page 14: CRACKING CONUNDRUM

1. French
2. Pesto
3. Toast
4. Inventing
5. Shed
6. Tea
7. Grand
8. Shaun

Answer=Feathers

Page 14: CHEESY PICKLE

Cheddar
Stilton
Edam
Mozzarella
Wensleydale
Cheshire
Brie
Red Leicester

Page 36: SOMEONE'S BEEN AT ME CHEESE!
Answer=Shaun the Sheep!

Page 38: TEST YOUR WALLACE & GROMIT KNOWLEDGE

1. [c]	6. [a]
2. [b]	7. [a]
3. [a]	8. [c]
4. [b]	9. [b]
5. [c]	10. [c]

Page 54: SCRAMBLED CHEESE ON TOAST

There are THREE cheeses on the toast!

●

Page 54: WENDOLENE'S WOOLY WIND-UP!

WALLACE matches THE CRACKER

GROMIT matches THE BONE

PRESTON matches THE GEARS

WENDOLENE matches THE BALL OF WOOL

SHAUN matches THE CHEESE

●

Page 55: PC MACKINTOSH'S SLEUTHOKU

1	3	2	4
4	2	1	3
3	1	4	2
2	4	3	1

Page 55: WALLACE'S TEA-BREAK CROSSWORD

	J			P	L	A	N	E			B		
H	A	M	M	E	R				T	R	O	U	S	E	R	S
	M		O	S							I		
D	A	Y	O	U	T			G	E	N	I	U	S
			R	T			G				T		
N		B	U	N	V	A	C				S		F
O		I		D			N	M				E
R	O	C	K	E	T			D	O			A
T		E		T				O		W		T
H			M	A	C	K	I	N	T	O	S	H
E				U			O	L		E
N	M	C	G	R	A	W				R
D				U						S
	W	E	R	E	R	A	B	B	I	T

59